Disney's

My Very First Winnie the Pooh™

Pooh's Favorite Singing Games

Compiled by Cassandra Case

GROLIER
BOOKS

BOOK CLUB EDITION

First published by Disney Press, New York, NY
This edition published by Grolier Books, ISBN: 0-7172-8902-8
Grolier Books is a division of Grolier Enterprises, Inc.

One fine day, after spending a lovely lunch comparing honey from different honey pots, Pooh decided it was time to do his stoutness exercises. While he stretched, he caught sight of himself in the mirror, and this funny little song popped into his head:

I'm a Little teapot

I'm a little teapot, short and stout.
Here is my handle, here is my spout.
When I get all steamed up, hear me shout,
"Just tip me over and pour me out."

"**O**h my, that was fun!" Pooh giggled. "And I do look rather like a teapot, so I'd better do some more exercises. How did the one that Christopher Robin taught me go? . . . Oh, yes!" And he sang:

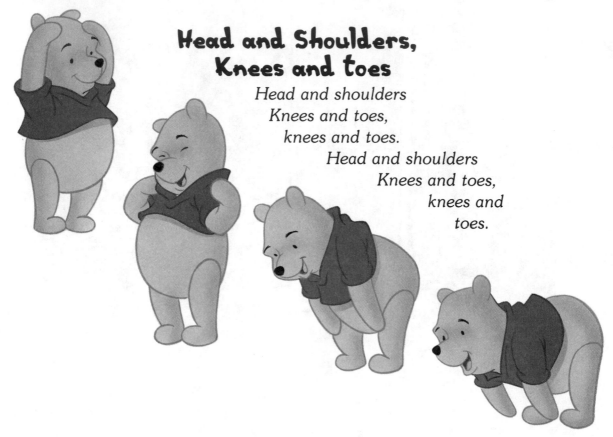

Head and Shoulders, Knees and toes

Head and shoulders
Knees and toes,
knees and toes.
Head and shoulders
Knees and toes,
knees and
toes.

Eyes and ears and
mouth and nose.
Head and shoulders,
Knees and toes,
knees and toes.

Pooh got through the whole thing all by himself. Then he thought, "This would be much more fun with two. I think I'll go find Piglet!" So he did.

Pooh found Piglet at home and showed him how to do the game. Piglet thought it was wonderful fun!

"Oh, I know another one!" said Piglet. "Do you know this one?" And he sang:

teddy Bear

Teddy bear, teddy bear, turn around,
Teddy bear, teddy bear, touch the ground.
Teddy bear, teddy bear, touch your shoe,
Teddy bear, teddy bear, that will do!

then Pooh found some old clothes that Christopher Robin had been planning to use to make a scarecrow for Rabbit's garden.

"This gives me an idea!" said Pooh. So he put them on and acted out this song:

Old MacDonald

Old MacDonald had a farm,
 E-I-E-I-O.
And on this farm he had a pig,
 E-I-E-I-O.
With an oink oink here
 And an oink oink there
  Here an oink, there an oink,
   Everywhere an oink oink,
    Old MacDonald had a farm,
     E-I-E-I-O.

Piglet joined in to do the "oinks."

"But," he said timidly, "if you don't mind, Pooh, I think I won't do the rest of the farm animals – especially not anything so big as a horse or a cow!"

Instead, Piglet showed Pooh a hand-clap game he liked. After some beginning fumbles, Pooh got through this whole song without one mistake:

Miss Mary Mack

Miss Mary Mack, Mack, Mack,
All dressed in black, black, black,
With silver buttons, buttons, buttons,
All down her back, back, back.

She asked her mother, mother, mother,
For fifteen cents, cents, cents,
To see the elephant, elephant, elephant,
Jump over the fence, fence, fence.

He jumped so high, high, high,
He touched the sky, sky, sky,
And didn't come back, back, back,
Until the fourth of July, -ly, -ly.

Just as they were finishing the third time through, Kanga and Roo happened along. Roo asked Kanga to do one of their favorite games – the one that always made him giggle (because it tickles!)

So Kanga taught them this:

Open, Shut them

Open, shut them, open, shut them,
  give a little clap.
Open, shut them, open, shut them,
  lay them in your lap.
Creep them, creep them, creep them,
  creep them right
  up to your chin.
Open wide your
  little mouth,
  but do not
  let them in.

the "creep, creep, creep" part reminded Pooh and Piglet of another one they knew, so they showed Roo how to play this singing game:

the Itsy - Bitsy Spider

The itsy-bitsy spider went up the waterspout.

Down came the rain and washed the spider out.

Out came the sun and dried up all the rain.

And the itsy-bitsy spider went up the spout again.

"**H**oo, hoo, hoo, hoo!" cried Tigger, bouncing up to his friends. "Looky who I found – our pal Christopher Robin! . . . Hey! Whatcha doin'? Can I play?"

"Come on, Tigger," said Christopher Robin. "Let's show them the game we learned the other day!"

It went like this:

Where Is thumbkin?

Where is thumbkin?
Where is thumbkin?
Here I am, here I am.
How are you today, sir?
Very well, I thank you.
Run away, run away.

"Oh, there you are!" said Rabbit. "I thought I heard laughing! I've been looking all over for you, Pooh. I need to borrow some soap to do my wash."

"Oh, ho!" said Christopher Robin. "Your wash can be part of the game!"

So he and Rabbit did the job while they sang:

this Is the Way We Wash Our Clothes

This is the way we
  wash our clothes,
  wash our clothes,
  wash our clothes.
This is the way we
  wash our clothes,
  so early in the
  morning.

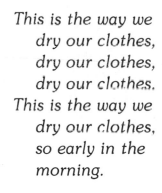

This is the way we
  dry our clothes,
  dry our clothes,
  dry our clothes.
This is the way we
  dry our clothes,
  so early in the
  morning.

Christopher Robin decided to go get Eeyore so he wouldn't feel left out. While the rest of them were waiting, Owl flew down.

"I was flying by and noticed what fun you were having," Owl said. "May I show you another wonderful game I know?"
They all agreed. It went like this:

London Bridge

London Bridge is falling down,
*   falling down, falling down.*
London Bridge is falling down,
*   my fair lady.*
Take the key and lock him up,
*   lock him up, lock him up.*
Take the key and lock him up,
*   my fair lady.*

Soon Christopher Robin returned with Eeyore.
"Hey, Eeyore, ol' buddy!" cried Tigger. "I know
a game that'll really cheer you up!"

If You're Happy and You Know It

If you're happy and you know it,
    clap your hands. Clap, clap.
If you're happy and you know it,
    clap your hands. Clap, clap.
If you're happy and you know it,
    Then your face will surely show it,
If you're happy and you know it,
    clap your hands. Clap, clap.

If you're happy and you know it,
    stamp your feet. Stamp, stamp.
If you're happy and you know it,
    stamp your feet. Stamp, stamp.
If you're happy and you know it,
    Then your face will surely show it,
If you're happy and you know it,
    stamp your feet. Stamp, stamp.

If you're happy and you know it, nod your head.
  Nod, nod.
If you're happy and you know it, nod your head.
  Nod, nod.
If you're happy and you know it, then your
  face will surely show it,
If you're happy and you know it, nod
  your head. Nod, nod.

If you're happy and you know it,
  pat your knees. Pat, pat.
  If you're happy and you know it,
    pat your knees. Pat, pat.
    If you're happy and you
    know it,
    Then your face will surely
    show it,
      If you're happy and you
      know it,
      pat your knees. Pat, pat.

"**t**hat's the happiest happy song I know," said Tigger.

"Oh, but wait!" said Christopher Robin. "Here's another one:"

the Wheels on the Bus

The wheels on the bus go round and round,
round and round, round and round.
The wheels on the bus go round and round,
All through the town.

The baby on the bus goes wah-wah-wah,
wah-wah-wah, wah-wah-wah.
The baby on the bus goes wah-wah-wah,
All through the town.

The lights on the bus go blink-blink-blink,
blink-blink-blink, blink-blink-blink.
The lights on the bus go blink-blink-blink,
All through the town.

The driver on the bus says,
"Move on back,
move on back, move on back."
The driver on the bus says
"Move on back,"
All through the town.

The money on the bus goes clink clink-clink,
clink-clink-clink, clink-clink-clink.
The money on the bus goes clink-clink-clink,
All through the town.

The people on the bus go up and down,
    up and down, up and down.
The people on the bus go up and down,
    All through the town.

The wipers on the bus go swish-swish-swish,
  swish-swish-swish, swish-swish-swish.
The wipers on the bus go swish-swish-swish,
  All through the town.

When they had finished, a loud, rumbly sound came from Pooh's tummy.

"Oh my!" said Pooh. "All this fun has made me hungry."

"We can all go to my house!" chirped Piglet. "I'll make us supper."

So off they marched for a friendly supper, singing all the way.

Yankee Doodle

Oh, Yankee Doodle went to town,
A-riding on a pony;
He stuck a feather in his cap
And called it macaroni.
Yankee Doodle keep it up;
Yankee Doodle Dandy,
Mind the music
and the step,
And with the girls
be handy.

After supper, everyone left except Pooh.

"Piglet," he said, "I have one last rhyme for you before you go to sleep:"

Little Green Frog

Ah – ump, went the little green frog one day.
Ah – ump, went the little green frog.
Ah – ump, went the little green frog one day.
And his green eyes went blink, blink, blink.

And that's exactly what Piglet's eyes did just before he dropped off to sleep.

Pooh went home and had a bubbly bath before he also went to bed. It had been such a fun day! So he hummed one last song, just for himself:

Little Duckie Duddle

Little Duckie Duddle
Went wading in a puddle,
Went wading in a puddle quite small.
Said he, "It doesn't matter
How much I splash and splatter,
I'm only a duckie, after all.
Quack, quack."